Why Why Why

does my heart begin to race?

Miles Kelly

PUBLISHING

First published in 2005 by
Miles Kelly Publishing Ltd
Bardfield Centre, Great Bardfield, Essex, CM7 4SL

Copyright © Miles Kelly Publishing Ltd 2005

2 4 6 8 10 9 7 5 3

Editorial Director
Belinda Gallagher

Art Director
Jo Brewer

Editorial Assistant
Amanda Askew

Author
Chris Oxlade

Volume Designer
Jo Brewer

Indexer
Helen Snaith

Production Manager
Elizabeth Brunwin

Scanning and Reprographics
Anthony Cambray, Mike Coupe, Ian Paulyn

ISBN 1-84236-605-X

Printed in China

British Library Cataloguing-in-Publication Data
A catalogue record for this book is available
from the British Library

www.mileskelly.net
info@mileskelly.net

Contents

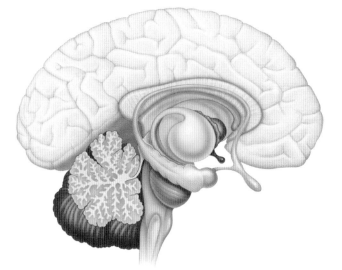

Why do babies grip so tightly?

Tiny babies can do simple things. If something touches a baby's cheek, it turns its head and tries to suck. If something touches the baby's hand, it grips tightly. These actions are called reflexes. They help the baby survive.

Giant baby!
A baby grows quickly before it is born. If it grew this fast for 50 years, it would be taller than Mount Everest!

Baby gripping

When do babies start to walk?

When they are about one year old. Babies can roll over at three months. At six months, they can sit up. At nine months they start to crawl. Then babies learn to stand and take their first steps.

Children playing

Am I always learning?

Yes, you are! Most children start school when they are five years old. They learn to count, read, write, and draw. Children learn outside of the classroom, too. Playing and having fun with friends is a great way to learn new things!

Find out

Find out three reasons why a newborn baby cries? Ask a grown-up if you need any help.

What does my skin do?

Skin protects you from bumps and scratches. It stops your body from drying out, and prevents germs from getting in. When you play on bikes or skateboards, you should wear gloves and knee pads to protect your skin.

Knee pads protect from cuts

Gloves protect from scrapes

Ouch! Ouch! Ouch!

There are millions of tiny touch sensors in your skin. They tell your brain when something touches your skin. Some sensors feel hot and cold. Others feel pain. Ouch!

Hair

Layers of the skin

Epidermis

Dermis

Touch sensor

How thick is my skin?

Your skin is very thin. It is only 2 millimeters thick. On top is a layer of tough, dead cells called the epidermis. These cells gradually rub off. New cells grow underneath to replace them. Underneath is another layer of skin called the dermis. This contains areas that give you your sense of touch.

Think

If you are riding a bike or playing on a skateboard, what should you wear on your head, and why?

Why do I sweat when I'm warm?

To cool down again. Your body warms up on a hot day or when you run about. You sweat to get rid of the heat. Your body lets sweat out through your skin. As the sweat dries, it takes away heat. This cools you down.

How much hair do I have?

Your whole body is covered in about five million hairs! You have about 100,000 hairs on your head. Hair grows out of tiny pits in your skin, called follicles. Hair grows in different colors and it can be wavy, curly, or straight.

Blonde wavy hair

Red straight hair

Black straight hair

Black curly hair

For the chop!

The hair on your head grows about 2 millimeters a week. If a hair is never cut, it reaches about 3 feet in length before it falls out. It is replaced by a new hair.

What are nails made from?

Fingernails and toenails are made from a hard material called keratin. It is the same material that hair is made from. Nails grow out of the nail root. In a week, a nail grows by about half a millimeter. They grow faster at night than in the day!

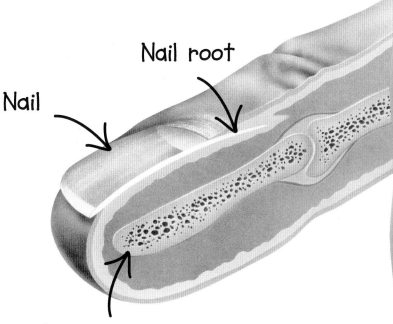

Nail

Nail root

Finger bone

Look

Have a look in the mirror. Is your hair straight, wavy, or curly? Use the pictures on page 8 to help you.

Why do we have fingernails?

Fingernails protect your fingertips. The nail stops your fingertip bending back when you touch something. This helps your fingers to feel things. Nails are useful for picking up tiny objects.

How many bones do I have?

Most people have 206 bones. Half of them are in your hands and feet. All your bones together make up your skeleton. The skeleton is like a frame. It holds up the other parts of your body. It also protects the squashy bits inside.

Find

Can you find your collarbone? It starts at your shoulder and runs to the top of your rib cage.

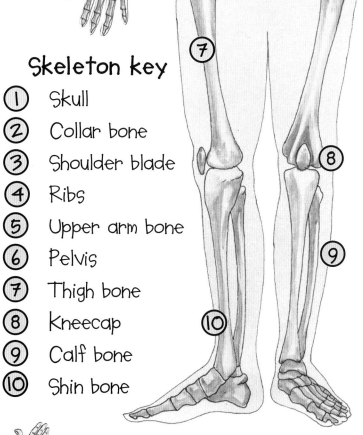

Skeleton key

1. Skull
2. Collar bone
3. Shoulder blade
4. Ribs
5. Upper arm bone
6. Pelvis
7. Thigh bone
8. Kneecap
9. Calf bone
10. Shin bone

What are bones made from?

Bones are made from different materials mixed together. Some of the materials are very hard and some are tough and bendy. Together they make bones very strong. There is a kind of jelly called marrow inside some bones. This makes tiny parts for your blood, called red and white cells.

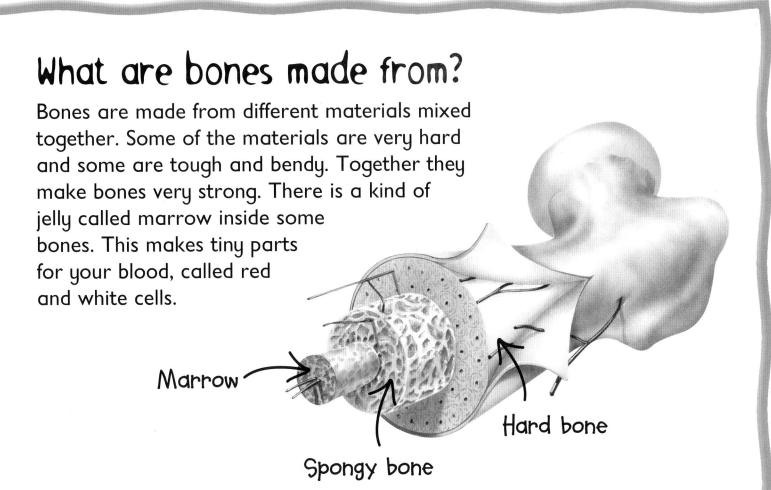

Marrow

Spongy bone

Hard bone

Strong bones!

Your bone is lightweight but super-strong. It is stronger than concrete or steel, which are used for making buildings and bridges! But bones can still break if they are bent too much.

How are bones joined together?

Your bones are connected by joints. They let your back, arms, legs, fingers, and toes move. You have about 100 joints. The largest joints are in your hips and knees. The smallest joints are inside your ear.

How do muscles work?

Muscles are made from fibers that look like bits of string. The fibers get shorter to make the muscle pull. Many muscles make your bones move. They help you to run, jump, hold, and lift things. Some muscles move your eyes, your heart, and other body parts.

Muscle fiber

Nerve

What is my biggest muscle?

The biggest muscles in your body are the ones that you sit on—your bottom! You use them when you walk and run. The strongest muscle in your body is in your jaw. It scrunches your teeth together.

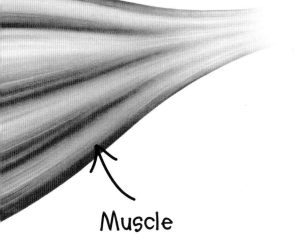

Muscle

What makes my muscles move?

Your brain does. It sends messages along nerves to your muscles. Lots of muscles are needed, even for small movements, like writing with a pen. Your brain controls other muscles without you thinking about it. For example, the muscles in your heart keep working even when you are asleep.

Why do I need to breathe?

You breathe to take air into your body. There is a gas in the air called oxygen that your body needs to work.

The air goes up your nose or into your mouth. Then it goes down a tube called the windpipe and into your lungs.

1. Air goes into your nose or mouth

2. Air goes down the windpipe

3. Air enters the lungs

Count

How many times do you breathe in and out in one minute?

Is my voice kept in a box?

Not quite! The real name for your voicebox is the larynx. It's at the top of the windpipe, and makes a bulge at the front of your neck. Air passing through the voicebox makes it shake, or vibrate. This is the sound of your voice. Your voice can make lots of sounds, and helps you to sing!

Singing

What makes air go into my lungs?

There is a big muscle under your lungs that moves down. More muscles make your ribs move out. This makes your lungs bigger. Air rushes into your lungs to fill the space. When your muscles relax, the air is pushed out again.

Fill 'em up!

When you are resting, you take in enough air to fill a can of soda in every breath. When you are running, you breathe in ten times as much air.

What food is good for me?

Lots of food is good for you! Different foods give your body the goodness it needs. Fruit and vegetables are very good for you. Bread and pasta give you energy. Small amounts of fat, such as cheese, keep your nerves healthy. Chicken and fish keep your muscles strong.

Fats keep nerves healthy

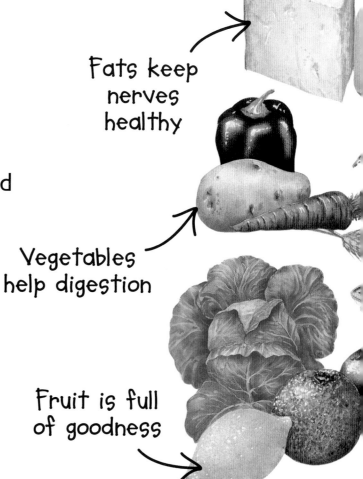

Vegetables help digestion

Fruit is full of goodness

Eating elephants!

You eat about 2 pounds of food every day. During your life, you will eat about 30 tons of food. That's the same weight as six elephants!

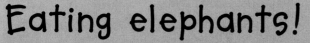

Bread gives energy

Fish helps muscles to grow strong

Why do I need to eat food?

Food keeps your body working. It is like fuel for your body. It keeps your body going through the day and night, and works your muscles. Food also contains things your body needs to grow, repair itself, and fight illness.

Your whole body needs food

What happens when I swallow?

The first thing you do with food is chew it. Then you swallow lumps of the chewed food. When you swallow, the food goes down a tube called the gullet. Muscles in the gullet push the food down into your stomach.

Draw

Look at some of the pictures on these pages. Can you draw a healthy meal that you would like to eat?

What are teeth made of?

Teeth are covered in a material called enamel. This is harder than most kinds of rock! Teeth are fixed into your jaw bones by roots. Sharp front teeth (incisors) bite food into small pieces. Tall, pointy teeth (canines) tear and pull food. Flat back teeth (molars) chew food to a mush.

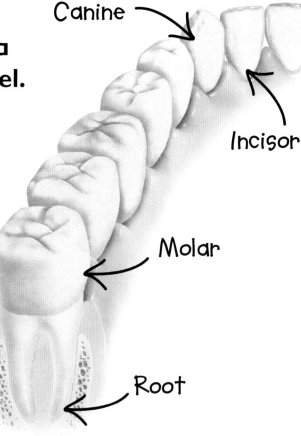

Canine

Incisor

Molar

Root

How many sets of teeth do I have?

You have two sets. A baby is born without teeth. The first set of teeth appears when a child is six months old. This set has 20 teeth. These teeth fall out at about seven years old. They are replaced by 32 adult teeth.

Discover

Do you still have your first set of teeth, or have your baby teeth begun to fall out?

18

Stomach

Large
intestine

Small
intestine

What happens to the food I swallow?

The food you swallow goes into your stomach. Here, special juices and strong muscles break the food up into a thick mush. The mushy food then goes into a long tube called the intestines. Here, all the goodness from the food is taken out, to be used by our body.

All gone!

When you go to the bathroom, you get rid of waste. This is leftover food. It is stored in your large intestine until you need to go.

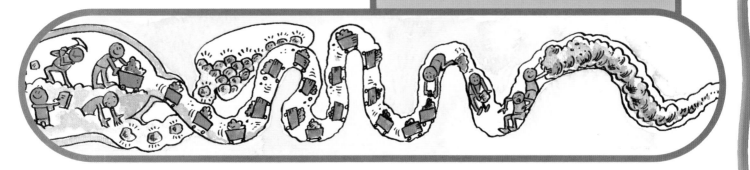

Why does my heart beat?

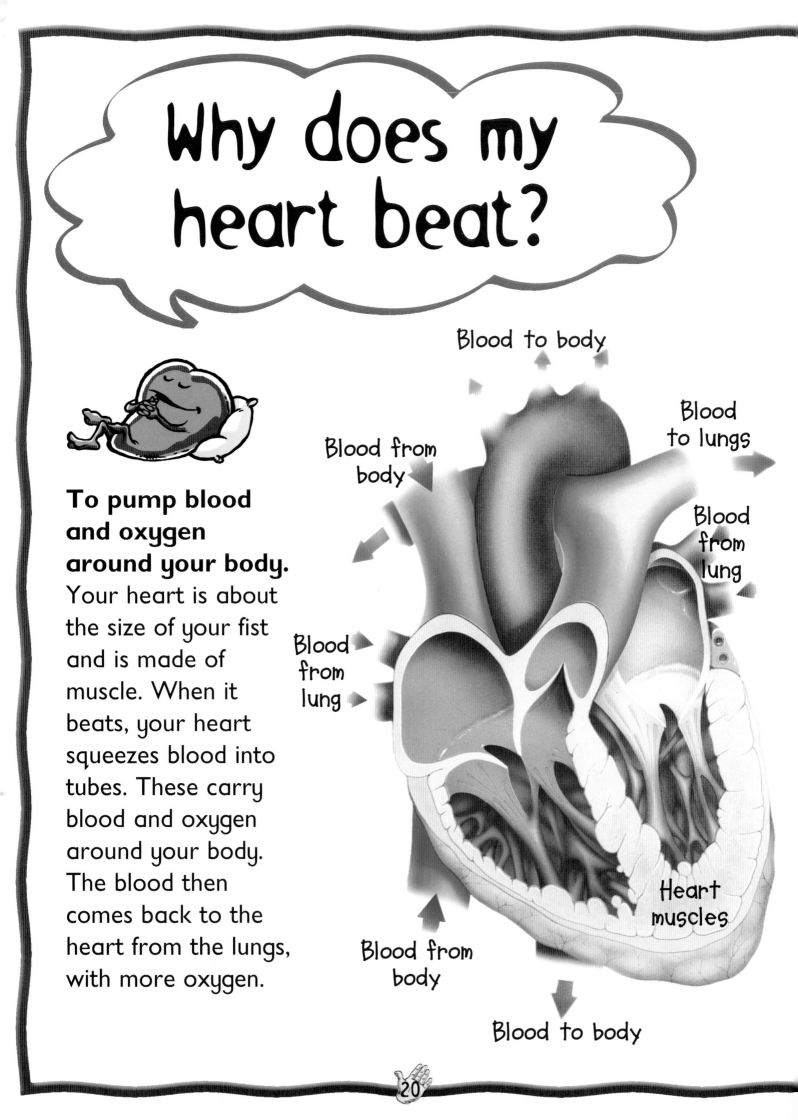

To pump blood and oxygen around your body. Your heart is about the size of your fist and is made of muscle. When it beats, your heart squeezes blood into tubes. These carry blood and oxygen around your body. The blood then comes back to the heart from the lungs, with more oxygen.

Blood to body

Blood from body

Blood to lungs

Blood from lung

Blood from lung

Heart muscles

Blood from body

Blood to body

Beat of life!

Your heart beats once a second for the whole of your life. That is 86,000 beats a day, and 31 million beats a year. In total, this is 2,000 million beats in your life.

What does blood do?

Your whole body need oxygen to work. Blood carries oxygen to every part of your body in its red cells. Blood also contains white cells that fight germs. Tubes called arteries and veins carry blood around your body.

Artery →

Red cell

White cell

Does blood get dirty?

Yes, it does. Because blood carries waste away from your body parts, it has to be cleaned. This is done by your kidneys. They take the waste out of the blood and make a liquid called urine. This liquid leaves your body when you go to the toilet.

Feel

Touch your neck under your chin. Can you feel the blood flowing through an artery to your brain?

Are my eyes like a camera?

Your eyes work like a tiny camera. They collect light that bounces off the things you are looking at. This makes tiny pictures at the back of the eyes. Here, millions of sensors pick up the light. They send a picture to your brain along a nerve.

In a spin!

Inside your ear are loops full of liquid. They can tell when you move your head. This helps you to balance. If you spin around, the fluid keeps moving. This makes you feel dizzy!

Lens collects light

Pupil lets light into your eye

Nerve to brain

Muscles make eye move

What is inside my ears?

The flap on your head is only part of your ear. The hole in your ear goes to a tiny piece of tight skin, called an eardrum. Sounds enter your ear and make the eardrum move in and out. Tiny bones pass these movements to the cochlea, which is shaped like a snail. This is filled with liquid.

Look

Look in the mirror at your eye. Can you see the dark pupil where light goes in?

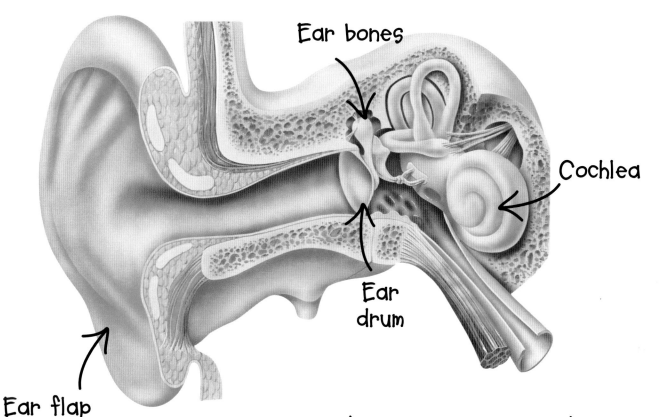

Ear bones

Cochlea

Ear drum

Ear flap

How do I hear sounds?

The cochlea in your ear contains thousands of tiny hairs. It is also is full of liquid. Sounds make the liquid move. This makes the hairs wave about. Tiny sensors pick up the waving, and send messages to your brain so you hear the sound.

Why can't I see smells?

 **Because they're invisible!** Smells are tiny particles that float in the air. Inside the top of your nose are sticky smell sensors. When you sniff something, the sensors collect the smell particles. They send messages to your brain, which tells you what you can smell.

Smell sensors

Nose

Bone

A blocked dose!
Smell and taste work together when you eat. Your sense of smell helps you to taste flavors in food. When you have a cold, your smell sensors get blocked, so you cannot taste, either.

How do I taste things?

With your tongue. Your tongue is covered with tiny taste sensors. These are called taste buds. Buds on different parts of your tongue can sense different tastes, or flavors. Your tongue also moves food around your mouth and helps you to speak.

Salty flavors are tasted here

Sour flavors are tasted here

Sweet flavors are tasted here

How many smells can I sense?

Your nose can sense about 3,000 different smells. You don't just have a sense of smell so you can smell nice things, such as flowers and perfumes! Your sense of smell warns you if food is rotten before you eat it.

Think

Look at the picture of the tongue. Can you think of three different things that taste sour, sweet, and salty?

Is my brain really big?

Your brain is about the same size as your two fists put together. It is the place where you think, remember, feel happy or sad—and dream. Your brain also takes information from your senses and controls your body. The main part is called the cerebrum.

Cerebrum

Right and left!

The main part of your brain is divided into two halves. The left half helps you to play music and to draw. The right half is good at thinking.

Cerebellum controls muscles

Brain stem

Can my brain really wave?

Well, sort of! Your brain works using electricity. It has about 10,000 million tiny nerve cells. Tiny bursts of electricity are always jumping around between the cells. Doctors can see your brain working by looking at the electricity with a special machine called an EEG. It shows the electricity as waves on a screen.

Remember
Your brain controls the five senses— smelling, tasting, touching, hearing— can you remember your fifth sense?

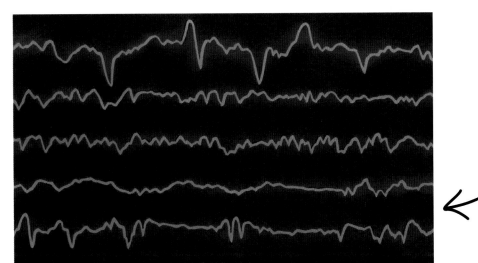

Brain waves from an EEG machine

How does my brain help me to play?

Different parts of your brain do different jobs. One part senses touch. Another part deals with thinking. Speaking is controlled by a different part. The cerebellum controls all your muscles. When you play and run, the cerebellum sends messages to your muscles to make them move.

How can I stay healthy?

There are things you can do to stop getting ill.  The easiest thing is to eat the right food your body needs, such as fruit and vegetables. Try not to eat too much food. Exercise such as riding a bike will keep your bones, muscles, and heart healthy.

Getting old!

Your body changes as you get old. You get shorter, your skin wrinkles and your hair might go grey. But you could live to be 100!

What can make me sick?

Lots of things can make you sick. Illnesses such as tummy upsets are caused by germs that get into your body. You can help to stop catching germs by washing your hands before eating and after going to the bathroom.

Washing your hands kills germs

Riding a bike can keep you healthy

Why do I have injections?

All children have injections at the doctors every few years. The injections help to stop you catching serious diseases in the future. Doctors also help you to get well again when you are ill. The doctor might give you medicine to make you feel better.

Read

Read this page again. What should you do before meal times and after going to the bathroom?

Quiz time

Do you remember what you have read about your body? These questions will test your memory. The pictures will help you. If you get stuck, read the pages again.

3. How much hair do I have?

page 8

page 5

1. Am I always learning?

2. Why do I sweat when I'm warm?

page 7

4. How are bones joined together?

page 11

page 12

5. How do muscles work?

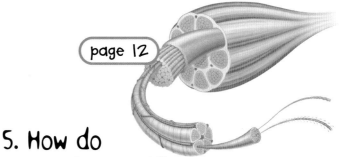

page 15

6. What makes air go into my lungs?

7. Why do I need to eat food?

page 17

8. How many sets of teeth do I have?

page 18

9. What does blood do?

page 21

10. How do I hear sounds?

page 23

11. How do I taste things?

page 25

12. How does my brain help me to play?

page 27

13. What can make me sick?

page 29

Answers

1. Yes, you are
2. To help you cool down again
3. You have five million hairs on your body
4. They are connected by joints
5. The fibers inside get shorter and pull
6. Muscles
7. To keep your body working
8. Two sets
9. Carries oxygen around your body
10. With the parts that are inside your ear
11. With your tongue
12. It tells your muscles to move
13. Germs

Index